The Internal Hygiene Journal

A 30-Day Guide to Self-Discovery and Wellness

Bertha F. Barrett, LMHC, LPC, CCTP

Copyright Page

No part of this publication may be reproduced, stored in a retrieval system, or transmitted in any form or by any means—electronic, mechanical, photocopying, recording, or otherwise—without the prior written permission of the author, except for the inclusion of brief quotations in a review.

For permission inquiries, please contact:
Intake Psychotherapy & Wellness, LLC
1415 Hwy 85 N. STE 310-394
Fayetteville, GA 30214

bertha.barrett@intakepsychotherapy.com
www.intakepsychotherapy.com

Disclaimer

The Internal Hygiene Journal is intended for informational and self-help purposes only. It is not a substitute for professional psychological, emotional, or medical advice, diagnosis, or treatment. The techniques, suggestions, and practices included in this journal are based on mindfulness, emotional regulation, and introspection principles. However, they are not intended to replace any professional guidance or therapy.

If you are currently under the care of a licensed mental health professional, medical provider, or counselor, or if you are experiencing significant emotional or psychological distress, please consult them before using this journal. This journal is not intended to diagnose, treat, or cure any condition, and any personal progress or emotional growth should be considered in conjunction with appropriate professional care.

By using this journal, you acknowledge and agree that the author and publisher are not liable for any outcomes, including emotional, mental, or physical effects, resulting from the use of this journal.

If you are in crisis or experiencing a mental health emergency, please seek immediate help from a licensed professional or contact your local emergency helpline.

CONTENTS

ACKNOWLEDGMENTS

To every client, past and present, who has entrusted me to walk alongside them in their healing journey: thank you. You've allowed me to witness the most sacred parts of the human experience—pain, truth, courage, and transformation. Through your willingness to sit with your discomfort, I found the inspiration to create this journal. You've taught me that presence is the greatest gift we can give ourselves, and that healing, though often messy, is always holy.

To my grandchildren—my brightest mirrors and most honest teachers—thank you for reminding me, daily, to stay present. You help me see how inner stillness becomes love in action. Your laughter grounds me, your curiosity humbles me, and your presence calls me deeper into my own. Because of you, I choose to constantly improve my inner world so I can show up fully in yours.

And most importantly, to God, my source, guide, and sustainer—thank You. Your Spirit continues to pour into me, even when I feel empty. Thank You for revealing, again and again, the beauty of returning inward. You have shown me that maintaining the internal self is not just essential but sacred. This journal is but a reflection of what You've revealed to me in the quiet spaces.

With gratitude and reverence,

Bertha

Journal Usage Guide: How to Use This Journal with Intention

🪶 Welcome Inward

Welcome to *The Internal Hygiene Journal*—a 30-day guide designed to help you reconnect with the most important relationship you'll ever have: the one with yourself.

This journal is not a test. It's not a fix.
It's a **daily invitation** to notice, feel, breathe, and reflect.
It's a practice of tending to your inner landscape the same way you care for your external one.

You brush your teeth. You bathe. You get dressed.
But what rituals do you have to clear emotional residue, regulate your nervous system, and tend to your inner voice?

That's where this journal comes in.
You're not here to become someone else. You're here to come home to yourself.

What's Inside

Each day of this journal offers a structured guide to create rhythm, not rigidity. You will find:

- Daily Intentions: To help guide and center your focus
- Affirmations: A simple truth to anchor your mindset
- Guided Practices: A trauma-informed, mindfulness-based activity to help you engage with your inner world
- Reflection Prompts: A writing invitation for emotional insight
- Self-Care Tips: A gentle, body-based way to support integration
- Self-Check-Ins: A quick, empowering way to assess how you're feeling
- Closing Reflection: A daily moment of closure, clarity, and acknowledgment

Every seven days, you'll find a Milestone Check-In—a chance to pause, celebrate growth, reflect on change, and gently course-correct if needed.

A Few Gentle Suggestions

1. **Go at your own pace.**
   This journal is designed as a 30-day practice, but that doesn't mean you must move directly from one day to the next. Some days may need more time, and some may invite a pause. Honor your rhythm.

2. **Keep it sacred.**
   Set aside 10–20 minutes a day. Light a candle. Play soft music. Journal in bed if you desire. Let this be your soul's appointment with you.

3. **There is no "wrong" way.**
   Some days, you'll write pages. You may struggle to write only a word or two on other days. Some days, you'll skip. Others, you'll cry. What's important to remember is that this is still the work.

4. **You are not alone.**
   If you feel overwhelmed, contact a therapist, mentor, or someone safe. This journal is a tool, not a substitute for support.

Why 30 Days? Why Internal Hygiene?

Because healing isn't a one-time act.
Just like external hygiene, emotional wellness **requires consistency**.

Research has shown that, for most behaviors, it can take anywhere between **2 and 5 months** to establish new behavioral pathways in the brain. This 30-day journey is your starting point—a foundational layer.

You're not here to complete something.
You're here to begin something sacred.
To say: *I matter. My inner world deserves attention.*
To remember that the emotional buildup we don't clean becomes self-doubt, anxiety, people-pleasing, or numbness, etc.

You're here to clear that space.
To prevent decay.
To stay connected to your wholeness.

Last Note Before You Begin

You are not a project.
You are not broken.
You are not behind.

You are closing the gap between who you were instructed to be, implicitly or explicitly, and becoming more aware of who you really are. And every page of this journal is a love letter to that becoming.

So, turn the page.
Take a breath.
And begin this journey inwardly—one honest, healing day at a time.

With reverence,

Bertha Freeman Barrett
Your Inner Wellness Guide

Introduction: Why This Journal Matters

If you've ever felt disconnected from yourself, this journal is your invitation home.

This is not just a journal—it's a sanctuary. It is a 30-day guided space designed to help you build the most important relationship you will ever have: the one with yourself. You're not here to fix who you are. You're here to remember, realign, and return inward.

Many of us were raised to prioritize the external—careers, relationships, appearances—but few of us were taught how to truly *tend to the internal*. I call this *internal hygiene*: the conscious practice of sitting with your thoughts, acknowledging your emotions, and witnessing what's happening within without judgment.

No one taught us how to be with ourselves. So, when you hear someone say, "Spend time with yourself," it may feel strange, awkward, or even threatening. Clients often ask: *What does that mean? What do I do? What am I supposed to feel?*

This journal is your starting point.

What Does It Mean to Sit with Yourself?

To sit with yourself is to gently turn inwardly—to quiet the noise of the world and listen, fully and kindly, to your internal experience. Just as we brush our teeth or shower to maintain physical cleanliness, sitting with yourself is a form of *internal hygiene*— it is a cleansing of your emotional and mental landscape.

When we neglect our internal world, it doesn't just go unnoticed. It shows up as racing thoughts, low self-worth, chronic stress, unconscious behavior, and even unexplained physical pain. As a clinical professional, I see the effects of unprocessed emotion daily. When your inner world is left unattended, it starts to clutter like any neglected space.

And just like external hygiene, when the internal is overlooked… things begin to stink.

But here's the truth: if stillness feels uncomfortable, you're not alone—and you're not broken. Many people carry trauma, conditioning, and emotional patterns that make stillness feel unsafe. That's okay. This journal will help you build safety gradually and gently.

The Benefits of Introspection

As you begin to sit with yourself, something profound happens:
You start to understand your mind and body from the inside out. You begin to observe instead of reacting. You make space for compassion instead of criticism.

Some benefits you may experience through this practice include:

- **Reduced Stress and Anxiety:** Quiet time supports nervous system regulation.

- **Improved Emotional Regulation:** You learn to meet emotions without pushing them away.

- **Increased Self-Compassion:** You stop judging your pain and start tending to it.

- **Enhanced Creativity and Problem-Solving:** Clarity grows in stillness.

- **Greater Sense of Self-Worth:** You realize your value does not require validation.

Introspection isn't about achieving some perfect emotional state. It's about presence, awareness, and intimacy with the self.

Why This Journal?

Think of *The Internal Hygiene Journal* as your guided companion—a sacred and structured space where you can practice inward attention. Over the next 30 days, you'll be guided through:

- Daily prompts

- Affirmations

- Gentle self-care practices

- Mind-body awareness tools

Each day builds on the last, creating a rhythm of self-connection. This journal isn't self-help in the traditional sense. This practice you are about to embark on is soul-maintenance.

If at any point the journey feels uncomfortable, that's okay. Growth often begins with discomfort. You're invited to move at your own pace. Use grounding tools, such as deep breathing, placing a hand on your heart, or noticing your feet on the floor, to stay anchored.

Getting Started: Your Intention

Before we begin, take a moment to set your intention. This small act anchors your practice in purpose.

Ask yourself:

- **What do I hope to discover about myself?**
  (Write below)

_____

_____

_____

_____

_____

_____

_____

_____

_____

_____

_____

_____

_____

- **How do I want to show up for myself over the next 30 days?**
  (Write below)

_____

_____

_____

_____

Now, close your eyes. Take a slow, gentle breath. Imagine stepping into a quiet room inside yourself—softly lit, safe, and still. This is your inner sanctuary. You are safe here. You are welcome here.

Let us begin—one day at a time.

Day 1: Building the Foundation

🍃 Daily Intention

Prompt: *What does being present mean to me today?*
(Write your reflection below.)

_____

_____

_____

_____

_____

_____

_____

_____

_____

_____

_____

_____

_____

_____

_____

_____

_____

Affirmation

"I am present and safe within myself."

Repeat this aloud or silently three times. Let the words sink in—not as a goal, but as a truth you are learning to trust.

Guided Practice: Sit with Yourself

Sit in silence for 10 minutes.

You don't need to empty your mind. You don't need to "do it right."
Just sit. Be. Notice. Breathe.

If it feels hard to be still, gently place a hand on your chest or belly and tell yourself, *"It's safe to be here."*
Let this practice be awkward, messy, and honest. You're building something new.

What Came Up?

What thoughts or feelings did you notice arise during your 10 minutes?
Don't edit. Just flow. Remember—no judgment, only observation.

_____

_____

_____

_____

_____

_____

_____

_____

_____

_____

_____

_____

_____

_____

_____

Today's Self-Care Tip

Take 3–5 minutes to practice deep, conscious breathing:

- Inhale slowly through your nose for a count of 4

- Hold for a count of 4

- Exhale through your mouth for a count of 6

Do this for a few cycles. This helps regulate your nervous system and signals to your body: *"I am safe."*

Self-Check-In

On a scale of 0–10, how difficult was it to sit quietly with yourself today?
(0 = Not at all difficult, 10 = Extremely difficult)
My number: _____

Optional: What made it feel that way?

_____

_____

_____

_____

_____

_____

_____

_____

_____

_____

_____

_____

_____

_____

_____

_____

Closing Reflection

What did you learn today about yourself, your mind, or your ability to sit still?

_____

_____

_____

_____

_____

_____

_____

_____

_____

_____

_____

_____

_____

_____

_____

_____

Day 2: Noticing the Body's Wisdom

🪷 Daily Intention

Prompt: *How does my body feel today? What is it trying to tell me?*
(Reflect below)

_____

_____

_____

_____

_____

_____

_____

_____

_____

_____

_____

_____

_____

_____

_____

Affirmation

"I listen to my body with compassion and curiosity."
Say this aloud or softly to yourself. Let the words land in your body—like medicine, not a mantra.

Guided Practice: Body Scan Awareness

Today, we gently shift focus to the body. Your body is a wise storyteller. It holds memories, emotions, tension, peace, truth, and resilience.

Find a quiet space. Close your eyes. Breathe slowly and begin to scan your body from head to toe. Gently notice:

- Where do I feel tension or tightness?
- Where do I feel calm or warmth?
- Are there any sensations that surprise me?

If you encounter discomfort, don't push it away— breathe with it. Let your body know: "I see you. I'm here."

Prompt: What Did You Notice in Your Body?

Write freely about the sensations, emotions, or images that surfaced during your body scan.

_____

_____

_____

_____

_____

_____

_____

_____

_____

_____

_____

_____

_____

_____

_____

Today's Self-Care Tip:

Stretch with Intention. Take 2-5 minutes to do a few mindful stretches. Focus on your breath and allow your body to move however it needs. You're not trying to "fix" anything–honor what is there.

Optional: End your stretch by placing both hands over your heart or belly and whispering: *"I'm listening."*

Self-Check-In

On a scale of 0–10, how connected did you feel to your body today?
(0 = Not at all connected, 10 = Fully attuned)
My number: _____

Optional: Where did you feel the most sensation?

_____

_____

_____

_____

_____

_____

_____

_____

_____

_____

_____

_____

_____

_____

_____

_____

_____

Closing Reflection

What did your body reveal to you today? Did any sensation surprise you, or feel familiar in a new way?

_____

_____

_____

_____

_____

_____

_____

_____

_____

_____

_____

_____

_____

_____

_____

_____

_____

_____

_____

_____

_____

Anchor Point for Tomorrow

Try closing your day with three deep breaths and a gentle body check-in before bed. A moment of inward attention can shift how we sleep, heal, and restore.

DAY 3: Meeting Your Inner Voice

🦋 Daily Intention

How am I speaking to myself today?

Affirmation

"My inner voice can be kind, wise, and gentle."

Soul Whisper: How you speak to yourself becomes how you experience life.

Say this out loud once and then whisper it softly. Let your nervous system feel the difference.

Guided Practice: Inner Dialogue Awareness

Take 5–10 minutes of silence. During this time, notice how your mind speaks to you.

- Are your thoughts critical or encouraging?

- Do they sound like someone from your past?

- Do you use "I" or "you" when speaking internally?

Tip: Imagine writing down your inner voice and then ask, "Would I say this to a child?"

Safety Note: If your inner voice is harsh or painful, please know this voice was likely learned, not born with you. It's okay to unlearn it, gently and slowly.

What Did You Notice in Your Inner Dialogue?

_____

_____

_____

_____

_____

_____

_____

_____

_____

_____

_____

_____

_____

_____

Today's Self-Care Tip

Write a short love letter or note of kindness to yourself. It doesn't have to be perfect—just heartfelt.

_____

_____

_____

_____

_____

_____

_____

_____

_____

_____

_____

_____

Self-Check-In

How would you rate the tone of your inner voice today (0–10)?
(0 = very critical, 10 = very compassionate)

My number: _____

Closing Reflection

What surprised you about your inner voice today?

_____

_____

_____

_____

_____

_____

_____

_____

_____

_____

_____

_____

_____

_____

_____

_____

_____

_____

_____

_____

_____

DAY 4: Making Space for Emotion

🌱 Daily Intention

What emotion have I been avoiding or carrying silently?

_____

_____

_____

_____

_____

_____

_____

_____

_____

_____

_____

_____

_____

_____

_____

_____

Affirmation

"All of my emotions are welcome here."

Soul Whisper: Even the emotions you hide carry wisdom and truth.

Guided Practice: Emotion Naming

Sit quietly and breathe. Ask yourself:

- *What emotion is most present in me today?*

- Where do I feel it in my body?

- Can I give it a name without judging it?

Then whisper to yourself:
"This, too, belongs."

Safety Note: If an emotion feels too big or overwhelming, return to your breath. Place your hand over your heart and say, "I am safe. I am here."

Write It Out: What Emotion Is Present?

_____

_____

_____

_____

_____

_____

_____

_____

_____

_____

_____

_____

_____

_____

_____

_____

What does this emotion want you to know?

_____

_____

_____

_____

_____

_____

_____

_____

_____

_____

_____

_____

_____

_____

_____

Today's Self-Care Tip

Use cold water therapy to regulate emotion—splash your face, hold a cool compress to your neck, or walk barefoot outside for a few minutes.

Self-Check-In

**On a scale of 0–10, how safe did you feel expressing your emotions today?
My number:** _____

Closing Reflection

What shifted for you after acknowledging this emotion?

_____

_____

_____

_____

_____

_____

_____

_____

_____

_____

_____

_____

_____

_____

_____

_____

_____

_____

_____

_____

_____

_____

_____

_____

_____

_____

_____

_____

_____

_____

_____

_____

Take a Soothing Pause

Before you move on with your day, take a moment to slow down and breathe.

This is your space to **rest, reflect**, and **reset**—not with words but color. Let your hands move freely. No pressure. No perfection. Just presence.

Color. Pause. Breathe.
Let this be your way of saying to yourself: *I am still here. And I am worth this moment of peace.*

Color. Pause. Breathe.
Let this be your way of saying to yourself: *I am still here. And I am worth this moment of peace.*

DAY 5: The Power of Stillness

🍃 Daily Intention

How can I give myself the gift of stillness today?

_____

_____

_____

_____

_____

_____

_____

_____

_____

_____

_____

_____

_____

_____

_____

_____

_____

_____

Affirmation:

"Stillness is where I remember who I am."

Soul Whisper: Silence doesn't mean emptiness—it means meeting yourself fully.

Guided Practice: Mindful Minute Intervals

Practice stillness in small intervals today. Set a timer for 1–2 minutes and do… nothing. Just breathe.

Try this **3 times** today:

- Morning

- Midday

- Before bed

Notice how it feels to pause or not reach for a distraction but to simply be.

Reflections on Stillness

- What thoughts or feelings came up during your mindful minutes?

- Did stillness feel comforting, restless, or something else?

_____

_____

_____

_____

_____

_____

_____

_____

_____

_____

_____

_____

_____
_____
_____
_____
_____
_____
_____
_____
_____

Today's Self-Care Tip

Take a digital pause: For one hour, avoid using your phone, screens, or notifications. Use that time to be with yourself, journal, or rest.

Self-Check-In

How did stillness feel in your body today (0 = very uncomfortable, 10 = deeply nourishing)? My number: _____

Closing Reflection

Did stillness reveal something you usually overlook?

_____
_____
_____
_____
_____
_____
_____
_____

DAY 6: Honoring Emotional Boundaries

🜂 Daily Intention

Where in my life do I need clearer boundaries to protect my peace?

_____

_____

_____

_____

_____

_____

_____

_____

_____

_____

_____

_____

_____

_____

_____

Affirmation

"I am allowed to protect my energy with loving boundaries."

Soul Whisper: Boundaries are not walls. They are bridges to healthier connections with others and with yourself.

Guided Practice: Energy Check-In

Today, notice where your energy feels most drained. Ask yourself:

- Who or what is pulling on my emotions?

- Have I been saying "yes" when I really meant "no"?

- Where am I abandoning my needs to avoid guilt, conflict, or rejection?

Then place your hand over your heart and say:
"I am learning to honor my needs without apology."

Safety Note: If boundaries feel hard, it may be because you were taught that love must be earned. Today, we unlearn that.

Prompt: Energy Awareness

Where have I been giving too much, or not enough, of myself lately?

_____

_____

_____

_____

_____

_____

_____

_____

_____

_____

_____

_____

_____

_____

_____

_____

_____

_____

What boundary(s) would bring more balance or peace into my life right now?

_____

_____

_____

_____

_____

_____

_____

_____

_____

_____

_____

_____

_____

_____

Today's Self-Care Tip

Say "no" gently but firmly at least once today—to an obligation, expectation, or mental pressure. Practice choosing yourself, even in small moments.

Self-Check-In

On a scale of 0–10, how empowered did you feel honoring your needs today?
My number: _____

Closing Reflection

What did you notice or feel after practicing one small boundary today?

_____

_____

_____

_____

_____

_____

_____

_____

_____

_____

_____

_____

_____

_____

_____

DAY 7: Milestone Check-In – The First Week Within

"Every time you check in with yourself, you reclaim a part of your wholeness."
— *Milestone Reflection*

Weekly Reflection Prompt

Take a breath. You've shown up for 7 days. That's no small thing.

Reflect below:

- What's one thing I've learned about myself this week?

_____   _____

_____

_____

_____

_____

_____

_____

_____

_____

_____

_____

_____

_____

_____
_____
_____
_____
_____
_____

- What was the most challenging part of this journey so far?

_____
_____
_____
_____
_____
_____
_____
_____
_____
_____
_____
_____
_____
_____
_____
_____
_____

- What's something I'm proud of, no matter how small?

_____

_____

_____

_____

_____

_____

_____

_____

_____

_____

_____

_____

_____

_____

_____

_____

_____

_____

_____

- Which prompt, emotion, or practice impacted me the most?

_____

_____

_____

_____

_____

_____

_____

_____

_____

_____

_____

_____

_____

_____

_____

_____

_____

_____

_____

Affirmation Review

Look back at the affirmations from Days 1–6.

Which one resonates most deeply with me today, and why?

_____

_____

_____

_____

_____

_____

_____

_____

_____
_____
_____
_____
_____
_____
_____

Emotional Landscape Check-In

Rate the following on a 0–10 scale (0 = not at all, 10 = fully):

- How present do I feel in my daily life? _____

- How connected do I feel to my body? _____

- How safe do I feel expressing emotions? _____

- How kind is my inner voice today? _____

Integration Prompt

What do I want to carry with me into the next 7 days?

_____
_____
_____
_____
_____
_____
_____
_____
_____
_____

_____

_____

_____

_____

Milestone Self-Care Ritual

Light a candle, drink tea slowly, journal freely, or take a walk—**intentionally mark this moment**. You're becoming someone who listens, honors, and loves themselves from the inside out

🖋 Optional: Letter to Self

Write a short letter to your future self—7 days from now. Offer encouragement, truth, and tenderness.

"Dear Me, this is what I want you to remember..."

_____

_____

_____

_____

_____

_____

_____

_____

_____

_____

_____

_____

_____

_____

Pause with Grace

You don't have to explain, fix, or process anything.

This is not a task—it's a gift.

Color slowly. Be still. You are enough in this very moment.

DAY 8: Reclaiming Self-Trust

🪶 Daily Intention

How can I show myself today that I can be trusted?

_____

_____

_____

_____

_____

_____

_____

_____

_____

_____

_____

_____

_____

_____

_____

Affirmation

"I trust my inner voice, even when it whispers."

Soul Whisper: Every time you follow through for yourself, your inner trust deepens.

Guided Practice: Honoring a Small Promise

Today, choose one small promise you can keep for yourself. It could be:

- Drinking a full glass of water

- Turning off your phone for 10 minutes

- Taking 5 slow breaths before reacting

As you complete it, say to yourself:
"I keep my word to myself."

Safety Note: Self-trust is often broken in environments where your needs were minimized or dismissed. Rebuilding it is sacred work.

Prompt: A Time I Didn't Listen to Myself

Write about a time you didn't trust your gut or silenced your inner voice.
What did you learn from that experience?

_____

_____

_____

_____

_____

_____

_____

_____

_____

_____

_____

_____

_____

_____

_____

_____

_____

_____

_____

_____

Now reflect: What's one way I can begin listening more deeply?

_____

_____

_____

_____

_____

_____

_____

_____

_____

_____

_____

Today's Self-Care Tip

End your day with a moment of acknowledgment. Write or say aloud:
"Today, I showed up for myself." Even if just in thought.

Self-Check-In

How strong did my self-trust feel today? (0–10)
My number: _____

Closing Reflection

What part of me felt more seen, heard, or trusted today?

_____

_____

_____

_____

_____

_____

_____

_____

_____

_____

_____

_____

_____

_____

_____

_____

_____

_____

DAY 9: Clearing the Mental Clutter

ᚖ Daily Intention

What thoughts have I been holding onto that no longer serve me?

_____

_____

_____

_____

_____

_____

_____

_____

_____

_____

_____

_____

_____

_____

Affirmation

"I give myself permission to let go."

Soul Whisper: Your mind is not a storage unit. You're allowed to declutter.

Guided Practice: Thought Dump

Grab a blank page and write nonstop for 5–10 minutes. Let it all out—fears, to-dos, judgments, random thoughts. Don't edit.

Once finished, circle or underline any recurring phrases or worries. Ask yourself:

- Is this mine, or something I've absorbed?

- Do I want to carry this forward?

Then whisper:
"I release what no longer belongs to me."

Safety Note: Mental clutter can be a form of emotional avoidance. Gently naming it allows your nervous system to release stored pressure.

Prompt: What thoughts or beliefs do I want to release?

_____

_____

_____

_____

_____

_____

_____

_____

_____

_____

_____

_____

Today's Self-Care Tip

Do a simple 5-minute tidy-up of a space—desk, bag, room corner. Physical space reflects mental space.

Self-Check-In

How mentally clear do I feel today? (0 = overwhelmed, 10 = spacious)
My number: _____

Closing Reflection

What did I learn about my inner thought landscape today?

_____

_____

_____

_____

_____

_____

_____

_____

_____

_____

_____

_____

_____

_____

_____

BERTHA F BARRETT

_____

_____

_____

_____

_____

DAY 10: Permission to Feel the Truth

🦋 Daily Intention

What truth have I been afraid to say—even to myself?

_____

_____

_____

_____

_____

_____

_____

_____

_____

_____

_____

Affirmation

"I am safe enough now to tell myself the truth."

Soul Whisper: Emotional hygiene requires emotional honesty.

Guided Practice: Write the Hard Truth

Choose one truth you've been avoiding about a relationship, a habit, a fear, or a dream. Write it.

Then ask yourself:

- What emotions does this truth bring up?

- What part of me needed this truth to be spoken?

Safety Note: Truth-telling doesn't mean self-blame. If any shame arises, pause, place your hand on your heart, and say: *"I deserve compassion here."*

_____

_____

_____

_____

_____

_____

_____

_____

_____

_____

Prompt: What truth do I need to hear from myself today?

_____

_____

_____

_____

_____

_____

_____

_____

_____

_____

_____

_____

What's one small step I can take to honor this truth?

_____

_____

_____

_____

_____

_____

_____

_____

_____

_____

_____

_____

Today's Self-Care Tip

Write a compassionate response to your truth, as if it came from a dear friend. Be kind. Be gentle. You're healing.

Self-Check-In

How emotionally honest did I allow myself to be today? (0–10)
My number: _____

Closing Reflection

What did my truth teach me today about who I am?

_____

_____

_____

_____

_____

_____

_____

_____

_____

_____

_____

_____

_____

_____

_____

_____

_____

_____

_____

_____

_____

_____

_____

_____

_____

_____

_____

DAY 11: Saying No from the Heart

🦋 Daily Intention

Where in my life do I need to say "no" to honor my "yes"?

_____

_____

_____

_____

_____

_____

_____

_____

_____

_____

_____

_____

_____

_____

Affirmation

"I can say no with love and still be worthy of connection."

Soul Whisper: Saying no creates space for a more aligned yes.

Guided Practice: Heart-Led Boundaries

Close your eyes. Place your hand over your heart. Take a few breaths.

Ask yourself:

- What am I tolerating that's weighing on me?

- What am I afraid will happen if I say no?

- What would honoring myself look like today?

Whisper to your heart:
"I give you permission to speak up for what you need."

Safety Note: If saying no feels unsafe, remember this is a skill learned over time. Even *noticing* where you want to say no is a victory.

Prompt: What does my heart want to say no to today?

What kind of connection would feel more honoring to me?

_____

_____

_____

_____

_____

_____

_____

_____

_____

_____

_____

_____

Today's Self-Care Tip

Say no to one draining request—mentally or verbally—and replace it with a small act of self-yes: a nap, a walk, a breath, or rest.

Self-Check-In

How empowered did I feel setting emotional boundaries today? (0–10)
My number: _____

Closing Reflection

What did I learn about how I protect or betray my energy?

_____

_____

_____

_____

_____

_____

_____

_____

_____

_____

_____

_____

_____

_____

_____

_____

_____

_____

_____

_____

_____

_____

_____

_____

_____

_____

_____

_____

_____

_____

_____

_____

_____

_____

_____

DAY 12: You Are Your Own Validation

🦋 Daily Intention

What if I didn't need approval to trust my path today?

_____

_____

_____

_____

_____

_____

_____

_____

_____

_____

_____

_____

_____

_____

Affirmation

"I am enough, even when no one claps."

Soul Whisper: Needing permission to be yourself is a cage you can walk out of.

Guided Practice: Reclaim Your Voice

Reflect on a time when you needed external validation (praise, agreement, applause). Now ask:

- What part of me needed to be seen?

- Did I abandon my truth to be accepted?

- What would I do differently now?

Then affirm:
"My truth matters—even if no one gets it but me."

Safety Note: The need for approval often comes from childhood patterns. Be gentle. You are rewriting your story now.

Prompt: Where have I been seeking external approval?

How can I offer myself what I was hoping to get from others?

Today's Self-Care Tip

Write your own praise today. Name 3 things you're proud of—just for you.

Self-Check-In

How self-validating did I feel today? (0–10)
My number: _____

Closing Reflection

What shifted when I chose to validate myself from within?

DAY 13: Caring for Past My Inner Wounds

🦋 Daily Intention

What part of the past is still coloring my present?

_____

_____

_____

_____

_____

_____

_____

_____

_____

_____

_____

_____

Affirmation

"I release the past to make space for my healing."

Soul Whisper: The past shaped you. It does not have to define you.

Guided Practice: Past-Present Check-In

Sit quietly and think of a moment from your past that still feels unresolved or heavy.

- What feeling still lingers?

- What belief did I form because of that experience?

- How does it show up in my present reactions or relationships?

Then say gently:

"I honor where I've been and am not stuck there."

Safety Note: This is tender territory. Pause anytime. Breathe. You do not need to resolve everything—just acknowledge it and be with it today.

Prompt: What experience from my past do I need to speak to today?

_____

_____

_____

_____

_____

_____

_____

_____

_____

_____

_____

What truth or closure does that younger version of me need to hear?

_____

_____

_____

_____

_____

_____

_____

_____

_____

_____

_____

_____

_____

_____

Today's Self-Care Tip

Write a short note to your younger self. Offer compassion, not correction.

"You didn't know. You were trying to survive."

Self-Check-In

How present did I feel today, even as I visited the past? (0–10)
My number: _____

Closing Reflection

What part of me felt lighter or acknowledged after today's reflection?

_____

_____

_____

_____

_____

_____

_____

DAY 14: Responding, Not Reacting

🜊 Daily Intention

How can I respond to my emotions instead of reacting to them today?

_____

_____

_____

_____

_____

_____

_____

_____

_____

_____

_____

_____

Affirmation

"I can pause, breathe, and choose my response."

Soul Whisper: The space between feeling and reacting is where your freedom lives.

Guided Practice: Trigger Mapping

Reflect on a moment today (or recently) when you felt **triggered**—angry, dismissed, anxious, defensive. Ask:

- What emotion rose quickly?

- What did I feel in my body?

- What did I want to do immediately?

- What would a *wise response* look like?

Then say:
"I'm learning to pause, not punish."

Safety Note: Triggers often come from past pain echoing into the present. Responding instead of reacting is a learned nervous system skill—be gentle as you practice.

Prompt: What tends to trigger me emotionally?

How can I meet myself with compassion instead of reaction in those moments?

_____

_____

_____

_____

_____

_____

_____

_____

_____

_____

_____

_____

Today's Self-Care Tip

Practice the **4-7-8 breathing technique** during stress:
Inhale for 4 seconds → Hold for 7 → Exhale for 8
Do 3 cycles when you feel overwhelmed.

Self-Check-In

How intentional was I with my emotional responses today? (0–10)
My number: _____

Closing Reflection

What did I discover about my emotional patterns today?

_____

_____

_____

_____

_____

_____

_____

_____

_____

_____

_____

_____

_____

_____

_____

_____

_____

_____

_____

_____

_____

_____

_____

_____

_____

_____

_____

Milestone Check-In #2 – Halfway Point

"You've done more than you realize."

Reflection Prompts:

- **What emotional habit have I shifted or softened this week?**
  Reflect on an emotional pattern or belief you've let go of, or something new you've embraced.

- **What has been the most challenging part of this journey so far?**
  Sometimes growth feels uncomfortable. Reflect on what has challenged you and how you've overcome it.

_____

_____

_____

_____

_____

_____

- **What progress can I celebrate today?**
  Take a moment to acknowledge any change you've experienced since starting this journal, no matter how small.

_____

_____

_____

_____

_____

_____

_____

_____

_____

_____

- **How do I feel about continuing this path for the next 2 weeks?**
  Check in with yourself and your sense of readiness for the next chapter of this journey.

_____

_____

_____

_____

_____

_____

_____

_____

_____

_____

_____

_____

_____

Self-Check-In:

Rate your emotional growth and self-awareness on a scale of 0–10.

My number: _____

DAY 15: Creating an Inner Safe Space

❦ Daily Intention

What does emotional safety feel like—and how can I give it to myself today?

_____

_____

_____

_____

_____

_____

_____

_____

_____

_____

_____

Affirmation

"I can create safety within myself, one breath at a time."

Soul Whisper: You are not broken—you just need to find your sanctuary within.

Guided Practice: Imagining Your Inner Sanctuary

Close your eyes. Imagine a real or imaginary space where you feel completely safe, unseen, and held. Visualize it in detail:

- What does it look like?

- What sounds do you hear?

- What textures or smells are around you?

- Are you alone, or with someone supportive?

This is your **internal safe place**. Return here whenever the world feels overwhelming.

Safety Note: If you struggle to imagine safety, try anchoring into your body: your breath, your heartbeat, your hands resting on your lap.

Prompt: What does emotional safety mean to me?

_____

_____

_____

_____

_____

_____

_____

_____

_____

_____

_____

_____

Describe your imagined safe place below:

_____

_____

_____

_____

_____

_____

Today's Self-Care Tip

Build a real-world comfort ritual: warm drink, cozy blanket, candle, favorite song—create a physical moment of internal refuge.

Self-Check-In

How emotionally safe did I feel with myself today? (0–10)
My number: _____

Closing Reflection

What was I doing, or thinking, when I felt most safe today?

_____

_____

_____

_____

_____

_____

_____

_____

_____

_____

_____

_____

_____

_____

DAY 16: Compassion Over Comparison

⚘ Daily Intention

How can I offer myself grace instead of comparison today?

Affirmation

"My journey is my own, and it is sacred."

Soul Whisper: You are not behind. You are becoming.

Guided Practice: Healing Comparison Triggers

Bring to mind a recent moment when you compared yourself to someone else (on social media, in your work, in your healing, etc.).

Ask:

- What did I believe they had that I didn't?

- What did I make that mean about me?

- What would compassion say in that moment?

Whisper to yourself:
"Their path is theirs. My path is mine."

Safety Note: Comparison often covers up old wounds of inadequacy or abandonment. Gently peel it back and meet what's underneath with kindness.

Prompt: What recent comparison left me feeling 'less than'?

_____

_____

_____

_____

_____

_____

_____

_____

_____

_____

_____

What would I say to a younger version of me who felt the same?

_____

_____

_____

_____

_____

_____

_____

_____

_____
_____
_____

Today's Self-Care Tip

Unfollow, mute, or distance yourself from one digital or social space that fuels comparison, and replace it with something nourishing.

Self-Check-In

How kind was I to myself in moments of comparison today? (0–10)
My number: _____

Closing Reflection

What truth did I remember about my worth today?

_____
_____
_____
_____
_____
_____
_____
_____
_____
_____
_____
_____

DAY 17: Learning to Self-Soothe

🦋 Daily Intention

What do I need today to feel calm and supported from within?

Affirmation

"I know how to comfort myself in moments of discomfort."

Soul Whisper: You don't have to wait for someone else to soothe you; you can be that someone.

Guided Practice: Soothe the Body, Soothe the Mind

Take a moment today to gently comfort yourself, especially when you feel tension or agitation.

Try one or more of these:

- Place one hand over your chest and one over your belly.

- Rock gently side to side while seated.

- Say a phrase out loud: **"I am here. I am safe."**

Then breathe slowly, letting your body feel your own care.

Safety Note: If self-soothing feels unnatural or silly, you're not doing it wrong. You're just giving your nervous system something it may have never had before.

Prompt: What does my body want from me when I feel anxious or upset?

_____

_____

_____

_____

_____

_____

_____

_____

_____

_____

_____

_____

What soothing action can I practice more regularly?

_____

_____

_____

_____

_____

_____

_____

_____

_____

_____

_____

Today's Self-Care Tip

Wrap yourself in a blanket, take a warm bath, listen to soft music, and give your body the signal that it is safe, seen, and held.

Self-Check-In

How well did I tend to myself in difficult moments today? (0–10)
My number: _____

Closing Reflection

What helped me feel more anchored today—and can I offer that again tomorrow?

_____

_____

_____

_____

_____

_____

_____

_____

_____

_____

_____

_____

_____

_____

_____

_____

DAY 18: Facing Shadow Emotions

ꙮ Daily Intention

What emotion have I been taught to hide or feel shame around?

Affirmation

"All parts of me—including the ones I fear—deserve my attention."

Soul Whisper: Your shadow is not your enemy. It's your unseen teacher.

Guided Practice: Naming What's Hidden

Choose a "shadow emotion" to explore today—anger, envy, bitterness, guilt.

Ask:

- Where do I feel this in my body?

- What does this emotion want to protect me from?

- What am I afraid others would think if they saw this side of me?

Then offer a reframe:
"Even this part of me is worthy of love and healing."

Safety Note: Shadow work brings up deeply buried parts of ourselves. You are not wrong for having these feelings. You are brave for turning toward them.

Prompt: What shadow emotion am I ready to acknowledge today?

_____

_____

_____

_____

_____

_____

_____

_____

_____

_____

_____

_____

What would it say if I let it speak honestly?

_____

_____

_____

_____

_____

_____

_____

_____

_____

_____

Today's Self-Care Tip

Do a cleansing release: cry, scribble, punch a pillow, dance wildly—move the emotion through, not around.

Self-Check-In

How safe did I feel acknowledging shadow emotions today? (0–10)
My number: _____

Closing Reflection

What truth or tenderness did this shadow emotion carry?

_____

_____

_____

_____

_____

_____

_____

_____

_____

_____

_____

_____

_____

_____

_____

_____

_____

_____

_____

_____

DAY 19: Joy as Internal Hygiene

🦋 Daily Intention

Where can I let joy into my day, even in small ways?

Affirmation

"Joy is the scent of my healing—it lingers long after the moment has passed."

Soul Whisper: You were never meant to heal in shadows alone. You deserve delight in your cleansing.

Guided Practice: Finding Joy in the Ordinary

Today, pause throughout your day to notice *one joyful moment at a time*.

This could be:

- A favorite song

- Sunlight on your face

- Laughter from someone nearby

- The smell of something comforting

Let the moment wash over you. Say aloud:
"This joy is mine."

Safety Note: If joy feels foreign, forbidden, or fleeting—go slowly. You may have learned to associate joy with fear of loss. You can unlearn that.

Prompt: What brought me a spark of joy today, however small?

_____
_____
_____
_____
_____
_____
_____
_____
_____
_____
_____
_____

How can I create or invite more of that into my life?

_____
_____
_____
_____
_____
_____
_____
_____

_____

_____

_____

Today's Self-Care Tip

Create a 3-song joy playlist and move your body to it, freely. Let joy be embodied. Let it perfume your internal world.

Self-Check-In

How much joy did I allow myself to experience today? (0–10)
My number: _____

Closing Reflection

What did today teach me about my relationship to joy?

_____

_____

_____

_____

_____

_____

_____

_____

_____

_____

DAY 20: Honoring the Progress, You Can't Always See

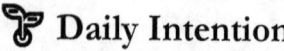 Daily Intention

What inner shifts have I made, even if no one else sees them?

Affirmation

"Healing is happening, even when it's quiet."

Soul Whisper: The invisible work is still real. Trust the roots before the bloom.

Guided Practice: Quiet Progress Inventory

Take 10 quiet minutes. Sit or lie down with your hand on your heart.

Ask:

- What am I doing differently now, compared to two weeks ago?

- What emotions do I allow myself to feel more freely?

- What parts of me feel softer, stronger, or more present?

Let the answers come without pressure. Some progress whispers before it roars.

Safety Note: If you feel discouraged or like "nothing has changed," that's okay. You're not behind. You're building capacity—and that takes time.

Prompt: What progress have I made that might be invisible to others, but meaningful to me?

_____

_____

_____

_____

_____

_____

_____

_____

_____

_____

_____

_____

What can I acknowledge myself for today?

_____

_____

_____

_____

_____

_____

_____

_____

_____

_____

_____

Today's Self-Care Tip

Do something small to celebrate your inner work—buy yourself flowers, take a solo walk, write yourself a thank-you card.

Self-Check-In

How connected do I feel to the progress I've made? (0–10)
My number: _____

Closing Reflection

What inner part of me feels seen, healed, or heard in a new way?

_____

_____

_____

_____

_____

_____

_____

_____

_____

_____

Milestone Check-In #3

"What You Can't Always See Is Still Sacred."

Take a breath. You've gone through 3 weeks of presence, truth, and emotional hygiene. You've tended to parts of yourself most people avoid—and that deserves to be witnessed.

Reflection Prompts:

- **What's one emotional habit I've gently shifted or softened this week?**

_____

_____

_____

_____

_____

_____

_____

_____

_____

_____

_____

_____

_____

- **What shadow or truth did I bravely acknowledge?**

_____

_____

_____

_____

_____

_____

_____

_____

_____

_____

_____

_____

_____

_____

- **What's something I no longer apologize for?**

_____

_____

_____

_____

_____

_____

_____

_____

_____

_____

_____

_____

_____

_____

- **What tool or prompt has helped me the most so far?**

_____

_____

_____

_____

_____

_____

_____

_____

_____

_____

_____

_____

Affirmation Review

Look back at Days 14–20. Which affirmation felt like a homecoming?

Write it again here, in your own words if you like:

_____

_____

_____

_____

_____

_____

_____

_____

_____

_____

_____

_____

_____

Emotional Tracking Recap

Rate yourself across the following (0 = not at all, 10 = deeply):

Category	Your Number
Presence in daily life	_____
Emotional safety with self	_____
Confidence in setting boundaries	_____
Capacity for self-kindness	_____
Ability to return to stillness	_____

Letter to Self (Optional)

Write yourself a message as if from a future version of you who has fully integrated everything you're learning.

"Dear Me, here's what I want you to remember..."

Breathe and Color

You've done meaningful inner work today. Let this be your exhale.
Let the colors speak when words feel tired.
Let stillness be enough.

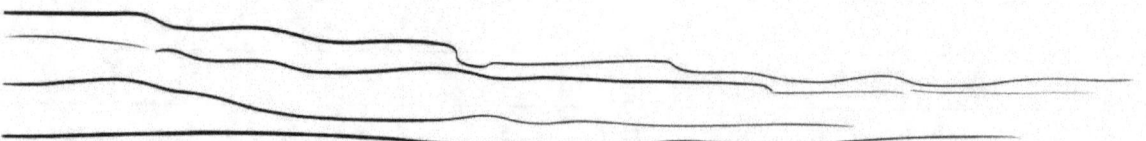

DAY 21: Who Am I Beyond My Roles?

 **Daily Intention**

Who am I when I'm not performing, pleasing, or proving anything to anyone?

Affirmation

"I am more than what I do for others."

Soul Whisper: You are a soul, not a role.

Guided Practice: Stripping Away the Shoulds

Take 10 minutes of stillness and ask yourself:

- If I weren't a partner, parent, healer, worker, friend… who would I be?

- What parts of me have been waiting for permission to emerge?

- When do I feel most like myself?

Write down a few honest responses and sit with them. Let your most authentic self rise gently.

Safety Note: If this feels confusing or confronting, pause and breathe. You've likely been conditioned to define yourself by service or survival. You are allowed to be whole for yourself.

_____

_____

Prompt: Who am I when no one is watching?

_____

_____

_____

_____

_____

_____

_____

_____

_____

_____

_____

_____

_____

_____

_____

_____

_____

_____

_____

_____

_____

What roles do I love—and which ones feel like cages?

Today's Self-Care Tip

Do one small thing today that is **just for you**. Not for usefulness. Not for performance. Just for joy or truth.

Self-Check-In

How connected did I feel to my core identity today? (0–10)
My number: _____

Closing Reflection

What truth did I reclaim about who I really am?

_____

_____

_____

_____

_____

_____

_____

_____

_____

_____

_____

_____

_____

_____

DAY 22: Redefining Success from Within

☞ Daily Intention

What does "success" mean when it's aligned with my soul, not society?

_____

_____

_____

_____

_____

_____

_____

_____

_____

_____

_____

_____

Affirmation

"My version of success is sacred and self-defined."

Soul Whisper: Let your definition of enough be your own.

Guided Practice: Inner Metrics of Success

Think of an area in your life where you've felt "not enough." Then ask:

- Whose definition of success am I using here?

- What pressure have I inherited that no longer fits me?

- What would success feel like—not look like—if I defined it on my terms?

Now write:
"For me, success feels like..."

Safety Note: Redefining success may bring up guilt or fear. Remember: alignment is not abandonment. You're allowed to outgrow old measures.

Prompt: Where have I been chasing someone else's version of success?

_____

_____

_____

_____

_____

_____

_____

_____

_____

_____

What does *soul-aligned* success look and feel like to me?

_____
_____
_____
_____

Today's Self-Care Tip

Celebrate a small, quiet victory today that no one else might notice—but that mattered to *you*.

Self-Check-In

How aligned did I feel with my values today? (0–10)
My number: _____

Closing Reflection

What old story of "not enough" can I begin to release?

_____
_____
_____
_____
_____
_____
_____
_____
_____
_____
_____

_____

_____

_____

DAY 23: Forgiveness as an Act of Freedom

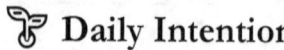 ## Daily Intention

What weight am I still carrying that I'm ready to lay down, not to forget, but to be free?

Affirmation

"I forgive so I can be free."

Soul Whisper: Forgiveness isn't letting them off the hook—it's letting yourself off the chain.

Guided Practice: Heart-Focused Forgiveness

Sit in quiet reflection. Consider someone (maybe even yourself) whom you've struggled to forgive.

Ask:

- What did I lose or feel when this happened?

- What have I been carrying since?

- What would it feel like to release that—not for their sake, but for mine?

Whisper:
"I'm allowed to set this down now."

Safety Note: Forgiveness doesn't mean reconciliation, trust, or denial. It means no longer letting pain be the author of your present.

Prompt: Who or what am I ready to forgive—not to excuse, but to release?

_____

_____

_____

_____

_____

_____

_____

_____

_____

_____

What does forgiveness look like *for me*—in action or energy?

_____

_____

_____

_____

_____
_____
_____
_____
_____
_____
_____
_____
_____
_____
_____
_____
_____
_____
_____
_____
_____
_____
_____
_____

Today's Self-Care Tip

Write a release statement and burn or shred it (safely). You might say:

"This story no longer defines me. I reclaim my peace."

Self-Check-In

How much lighter did I feel after practicing forgiveness today? (0–10)
My number: _____

Closing Reflection

What space opened up once I released what I no longer needed to hold?

_____

_____

_____

_____

_____

_____

_____

_____

_____

_____

_____

_____

_____

_____

_____

_____

_____

_____

_____

_____

_____

_____

_____

_____

_____

_____

_____

DAY 24: Boundaries in Relationships

 Daily Intention

What relationship dynamic needs more clarity, protection, or honesty today?

Affirmation

"My boundaries protect my peace and preserve my love."

Soul Whisper: Love without boundaries is not sustainable. Protection is connection.

Guided Practice: Energetic Relationship Audit

Today, take inventory of your emotional exchanges:

- Who do I feel energized after being with?

- Who do I feel drained, confused, or small around?

- Where do I stay silent to keep the peace?

Ask: *Where am I leaking energy that could be protected with clarity or distance?*

Safety Note: Boundaries don't make you cold—they make you clear. You're allowed to take up space in your own life.

Prompt: What relationship boundary do I need to express or reinforce?

_____

_____

_____

_____

_____

_____

_____

_____

What's one sentence I can practice saying to honor that?

_____

_____

_____

_____

_____

_____

_____

_____

Today's Self-Care Tip

Practice a boundary phrase out loud:

"I'm not available for that right now."
"That doesn't work for me anymore."
"Let me get back to you."

Your body will learn its strength even if you don't use it.

Self-Check-In

How empowered did I feel in my relationships today? (0–10)
My number: _____

Closing Reflection

What did I learn about where I overextend or override myself?

_____
_____
_____
_____
_____
_____
_____
_____
_____
_____
_____
_____

DAY 25: Creating Your Anchoring Ritual

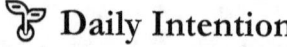 **Daily Intention**

What rhythm or ritual helps me return to myself when life pulls me away?

Affirmation

"I anchor myself with presence, not pressure."

Soul Whisper: You don't need discipline—you need devotion.

Guided Practice: Build Your Ritual

Today, design a short, simple ritual that reconnects you to *yourself*. Think:

- 5 deep breaths at your altar

- Morning tea in silence

- Saying an affirmation in the mirror

- Journaling by candlelight

- A grounding walk with hand on heart

The key? It's *consistent*, even if brief. Anchor in presence, not productivity.

Safety Note: Your ritual doesn't need to be perfect, aesthetic, or impressive. It only needs to *feel like you*.

Prompt: What kind of practice grounds me in my own energy?

_____
_____
_____
_____
_____
_____
_____
_____
_____
_____
_____
_____

What ritual can I commit to for 5 minutes a day?

_____
_____
_____

_____
_____
_____
_____
_____
_____
_____
_____
_____
_____

Today's Self-Care Tip

Choose one small ritual today and try it before bed. This will set the tone for a restorative, sacred night.

Self-Check-In

How grounded did I feel today through intentional rhythm? (0–10)
My number: _____

Closing Reflection

What felt sacred in the ordinary today?

_____
_____
_____
_____
_____

DAY 26: Owning My Desires Without Shame

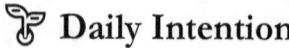 Daily Intention

What do I truly want—and where have I felt guilty for wanting it?

Affirmation

"My desires are not selfish—they are signals."

Soul Whisper: Desire is the divine trying to move through you.

Guided Practice: Naming the Want

Close your eyes and ask yourself:

- What do I sincerely, honestly want right now—emotionally, creatively, relationally, spiritually?

- What desire have I silenced out of fear, guilt, or shame?

- What might shift if I honored that desire without rushing to justify it?

Write it. Boldly. Lovingly.

Safety Note: If naming your desires feels unsafe, start small. Even saying "I want rest" is radical in a world that rewards overextension.

Prompt: What have I been taught is 'too much' to want—and how does that limit me?

_____

_____

_____

_____

_____

_____

_____

_____

_____

_____

_____

What would it feel like to want without apology?

_____

_____

_____

_____
_____
_____
_____
_____
_____
_____
_____
_____
_____
_____
_____

Today's Self-Care Tip

Do one thing today that honors a quiet want: a flavor, a color, a boundary, a craving for solitude, or a longing for joy.

Self-Check-In

How honestly did I acknowledge my desires today? (0–10)
My number: _____

Closing Reflection

What part of me came alive when I allowed myself to want without shame?

_____
_____
_____
_____

_____

_____

_____

_____

_____

DAY 27: Living in Alignment

ꙮ Daily Intention

What would it look like to live in complete alignment with who I am becoming?

_____

_____

_____

_____

_____

_____

_____

_____

_____

_____

_____

_____

_____

_____

Affirmation

"I honor the truth I've uncovered by living from it."

Soul Whisper: Awareness without action becomes stagnation. Alignment is love in motion.

Guided Practice: Alignment Mapping

Take a few minutes to reflect on what's shifted in your awareness these past weeks. Then ask:

- What am I doing, saying, or choosing now that feels aligned?

- Where do my actions still reflect old patterns or fears?

- What would *an aligned decision* look like today?

Let the answer rise from your gut, not your guilt.

Safety Note: Living in alignment is not about being perfect. It's about being honest. Even one aligned choice is a revolution.

Prompt: What does living in alignment mean to me now?

_____

_____

_____

_____

_____

_____

_____

_____

_____

_____

_____

_____

Where do I want to be more honest—with myself or others?

_____

_____

_____

_____

_____

_____

_____

_____

_____

_____

_____

Today's Self-Care Tip

Make one micro-aligned choice today. Say what you mean. Rest when you need. Choose what honors your truth—even if no one claps.

Self-Check-In

How aligned did I feel in my decisions and energy today? (0–10)
My number: _____

Closing Reflection

What did I learn about the space between knowing and doing?

_____

_____

_____

_____

_____

_____

_____

_____

_____

_____

_____

_____

_____

_____

_____

_____

_____

_____

DAY 28: Releasing What No Longer Fits

🌿 Daily Intention

What am I ready to release, not because it's bad, but because I've outgrown it?

_____

_____

_____

_____

_____

_____

_____

_____

_____

_____

_____

_____

_____

_____

Affirmation

"I am allowed to grow beyond what once held me."

Soul Whisper: Not everything you let go of is a loss. Some things are simply complete.

Guided Practice: Conscious Releasing

Write down anything you're ready to release:

- A pattern

- A role

- A thought loop

- A dynamic

- A fear

Then close your eyes and picture yourself placing it in a stream. Watch it float away. You are free.

Safety Note: Letting go doesn't mean forgetting. It means loosening the grip that keeps you feeling small.

Prompt: What am I no longer available for?

_____

_____

_____

_____

_____

_____

_____

_____

_____

_____

_____

_____

How can I lovingly close this chapter without shame?

_____

_____

_____

_____

_____

_____

_____

_____

_____

_____

Today's Self-Care Tip

Create a symbolic ritual today: release something physical (old clothes, paper, digital clutter) as a mirror for the energetic release.

Self-Check-In

How clear did I feel after letting something go today? (0–10)
My number: _____

Closing Reflection

What space opened up in me once I made room?

_____

_____

_____

_____

_____

_____

_____

_____

_____

_____

_____

_____

_____

_____

_____

_____

_____

WEEK 4 MILESTONE CHECK-IN

"I'm not the same person I was when I began—and that's something to honor."

Reflection Prompts

- What's something I've shed that I thought I needed?

- What's something I've reclaimed that I thought I lost?

- What is easier for me now than it was 4 weeks ago?

- What part of myself have I started to trust again?

Affirmation Review

Look back on the last week. Which affirmation do you want to stay with you after this journal ends?

Rewrite it here and make it your own:

_____

_____

_____

_____

_____

_____

_____

_____

_____

_____

_____

Integration Inventory

Rate your transformation across these areas (0 = not at all, 10 = fully):

Area of Growth	Score
Capacity to sit with emotion	_____
Boundaries and self-advocacy	_____
Self-soothing and emotional safety	_____
Trusting your inner wisdom	_____
Living in alignment with your truth	_____

Letter to the Self Who Began This Journey

Write to your Day 1 self as if they were your child, client, or closest friend:

"Thank you for being brave enough to begin..."

_____
_____
_____
_____
_____
_____
_____
_____
_____
_____
_____
_____
_____
_____
_____
_____
_____
_____
_____
_____
_____

DAY 29: Loving the Self As Is

🌿 Daily Intention

Can I meet myself today without trying to fix, improve, or edit anything?

_____

_____

_____

_____

_____

_____

_____

_____

_____

_____

_____

_____

_____

_____

Affirmation

"I am whole, even in my becoming."

Soul Whisper: Healing is not a race to a better version—it's a homecoming to your original self.

Guided Practice: Radical Self-Witnessing

Stand in front of a mirror or sit with your journal. Look into your own eyes.

Ask gently:

- What parts of me have I tried to hide or over-perfect?

- Can I offer compassion to the parts that still hurt, fear, or need?

- Can I let love meet me here, not once I'm "done," but _as I am?_

Then whisper to yourself:
"You are already worthy. Nothing more required."

Safety Note: Self-acceptance is a lifelong process. Today is not about arrival—it's about reverence.

Prompt: What would loving myself as I am look like today—in words, tone, or action?

What part of me is still waiting to be accepted?

Today's Self-Care Tip

Write a post-it note and place it somewhere visible:

"I am not a project—I am a person worthy of love, now."

_____
_____
_____
_____
_____
_____
_____
_____
_____
_____
_____
_____
_____
_____

Self-Check-In

How kind was I to myself today, even in imperfection? (0–10)
My number: _____

Closing Reflection

What shifted when I gave myself permission to *be*?

_____
_____
_____
_____

A Note Before You Turn the Page to Day 30

Dear Reader,

You've come so far.

You've listened inwardly. You've shown up on quiet days and messy ones. You've sat with yourself in stillness, in discomfort, in truth. And maybe for the first time in a long time… you've felt *seen* by the person who matters most: **you**.

Before you enter Day 30, let's take a sacred pause.

This work—this *internal hygiene*—is not meant to end here.
It was never about 30 days. It was about starting a practice that becomes a way of life.

Just like brushing your teeth, showering, or stretching your muscles… tending to your inner world is daily work. Emotional residue builds up. New fears emerge. Old stories return. Life keeps unfolding—and so do you.

And here's the truth:
As humans, we are constantly evolving, growing, grieving, and beginning again.
We experience new relationships, losses, transitions, successes, and each brings its own emotional

weight. Without inner care, we begin to decay in ways we don't always notice:

- Our self-worth erodes.

- Our clarity fades.

- Our joy gets buried beneath noise.

This journal may be closing, but *your work is not over.*
In fact, it's just beginning.

Change is built through consistency, not intensity.

Science shows that it takes **at least 2 to 5 months,** depending on the individual, to truly rewire behavior or create lasting internal habits. That's at least 5 months of checking in, recalibrating, sitting still, speaking kindly, and forgiving slowly.

That's six months of brushing your emotional teeth and washing your mental hands.

So please, don't stop here.
Keep returning to yourself.
Keep listening inward.
Keep clearing space for your truth, your peace, your voice.

Let internal hygiene become your rhythm.
Let it be the practice that protects your sense of self from the residue of the world.

And above all, remember:
You don't need to be perfect to be present.
You don't need to have it all together to be whole.

You just need to stay in a relationship with yourself.

With reverence,
Your future self
The one who will repeatedly thank you for not giving up on your inner world.

DAY 30: Integration + A Promise Letter to Self

 **Daily Intention**

How do I want to carry this version of me forward—gently, honestly, and with grace?

Affirmation

"This is not the end of the work. It is the beginning of the way I care for myself."

Soul Whisper: The journey inward never really ends—it just deepens.

Guided Practice: I Promise to Continue This Lifetime Journey

Light a candle or sit in silence for a moment.

Reflect on these questions:

- What has shifted in my heart, mind, or body?

- What patterns have softened or released?

- What new rhythm or ritual do I want to carry forward?

Then say softly:
"Thank you, Self. For staying. For showing up. For becoming."

Safety Note: Completion may stir grief. Let it come. You are not letting go of healing—you are integrating it into your life.

Prompt: What have I learned about myself in these 30 days that no one can ever take away?

What do I want to remember if I ever forget again?

_____

_____

_____

_____

_____

_____

_____

_____

_____

_____

_____

_____

_____

Today's Self-Care Tip

Write a promise love letter to yourself from your highest self. Let it hold you.

Your Becoming Letter to Self

Think of this letter as a lifelong unfolding of who you are and continue to become.

"Dear Me, you've come so far. Here's what I want you to hold onto as you continue your life's journey..."

_____

_____

_____

_____

_____

_____

_____

_____

_____

_____

_____

_____

_____

_____

_____

_____

_____

_____

_____

_____

_____

_____

_____

_____

Final Self-Check-In

Area of Growth	Start of Journey	Today
Presence with self	____	____
Emotional regulation	____	____
Self-compassion	____	____
Trust in inner voice	____	____
Living in alignment	____	____

Reflect on how far you've come—not in perfection, but in presence.

Final Reflection: A Life Lived Inwardly

"What does it mean to live in internal hygiene, every day?"

_____

_____

_____

_____
_____
_____
_____
_____
_____
_____
_____
_____
_____
_____
_____

What will your first *post-journal check-in* look like? Weekly? Monthly? In a moment of overwhelm.

Make a commitment:
"I will check in with myself again on..."

_____
_____
_____
_____
_____
_____
_____
_____
_____
_____
_____

_____

_____

_____

_____

_____

_____

_____

Reference

Singh B, Murphy A, Maher C, Smith AE. Time to Form a Habit: A Systematic Review and Meta-Analysis of Health Behaviour Habit Formation and Its Determinants. Healthcare (Basel). 2024 Dec 9;12(23):2488. doi: 10.3390/healthcare12232488. PMID: 39685110; PMCID: PMC11641623.

ABOUT THE AUTHOR

Bertha Freeman-Barrett is a compassionate Licensed Mental Health Counselor (FL) and Licensed Professional Counselor (GA) who specializes in trauma-informed care and emotional wellness. With a Bachelor's in Psychology and a Master's in Clinical Mental Health Counseling, she brings a holistic and culturally aware approach to mental health.

As a Certified Clinical Trauma Professional, Bertha helps individuals recover from trauma without reliving it. She is the founder and host of *The Intake Talk Show* on YouTube, where she tackles mental health stigma, cultural barriers, and emotional healing through powerful conversations.

Bertha is a passionate speaker, educator, and advocate for domestic violence awareness. Her work bridges the gap between clinical care and soulful self-empowerment, reminding us that true healing begins within.

"Your mind shapes your life—when you prioritize mental wellness, you create a foundation for living your best life."